# Linda's Diary:
# Feelings Galore

## Linda Chong

BookLeaf Publishing

India | USA | UK

Presentation by *BookLeaf Publishing*

Web: www.bookleafpub.com

E-mail: info@bookleafpub.com

ISBN: 9789357446402

First edition 2022

# DEDICATION

To the people of my past, present and future. If you're one of the cool ones who've managed to stick around, I dedicate this to you a little extra.

# ACKNOWLEDGE MENT

Thank you to everyone and everything that inspired my poetry. Both shitty and non-shitty.

# PREFACE

Dear No One,

I curse quite a bit, but it's a good time if you don't mind.

Sincerely,
Linda

# IT DOESN'T HAVE TO BE THIS WAY

Cunt, why?
Could you not?
No patience have I got—
For you, I have no time;
I think you're out of line.

Cunt, please.
Can you wait?
We are all running late—
Your parking fee does not concern me,
That is your responsibility.

Cunt, no.
There's no stock in the back,
But I'll 'check again' to appease you—
And no, there is not.
It seems I can never please you.

Cunt, wait.
Have you paid for that?
I saw you put it in your bag.
No, please, don't make this hard for me—

I'll have to call security.

Cunt, seriously.
I don't care,
Nor do I have more time to spare;
Your life story does not interest me,
I hope you leave this store quietly.

Cunt, really?
Do make up your mind,
There are other people waiting in line.
I am very tired and I have no room
For your fickle nature and mental decline.

Cunt, look.
My staff discount is only for me to use.
My employment here I cannot lose.

Cunt, honestly.
We have to close,
Most of us take public transport home.

# KFC

You are my KFC.
A crunchy coating that tempts me into bloating.

I am your seasoned lover.
Your umami mami.
Your greeter at the gates of my mouth,
And lover of your bones.

To lay with you in a soft tortilla wrap is the
most tender thing I could ever do.
A sweet glaze glistens with flavour on your
loins and tempts me with spices I cannot name.

Golden brown on the outside,
But it's what's inside that counts,
And you're beautiful.

I cannot resist your taste in my mouth.
A delightful feeling of lust down South.
I craved you last night,
Like you knew that I would.

I dreamt of you.
There was six of you.
Everyone wanted a piece,

But I got greedy and had you all to myself.

I love your rich history,
And the stories you tell;
Your meaty middle,
And chicken-y smell.

You are more than your crispy strips,
You are ranch, bbq and sweet chilli dips—
Oh shit.
I just came.

When the chips are down,
You're always around.
Warm, and hot when you want to be,
I knew it was Love I was feeling.

A moment on my lips,
A lifetime on my hips;
You make me feel like shit sometimes,
But I will never regret loving you.

# DO BETTER, GO DEEPER: A PENIS PERSONALITY TEST

Now that I've seen your penis,
I feel like I know a secret-
That's not so secret,
Because so many people have seen it.

Now that I've seen your penis,
I've never been more bored,
Because I never wanted to see it,
But you keep on sending more.

Now that I've seen your penis,
You want my opinion on your size.
Well, I wasn't looking all that hard,
So you must realise-
That it is not the size that counts.

If you wanted me to see your penis,
Then you should've said so.

You could've given me the heads up,
And I could've said no.

If you wanted me to see your penis,
I'd like to know for what reason.
Are you looking for approval?
Because this will end in deletion.

The truth is:
I don't think you deserve your penis.
Your penis is natural and stunning,
But you are kind of disgusting.

I didn't want to have to discuss these things,
But your behaviour is worth discussing.
Your personality is falling short,
And I want to know where things went wrong;
I wanna get the skinny, the fat and the long.

Please believe that your penis can't breathe
with all the pressure you put on it to be-
Something that it's not.

Someday there could be more between us
When you learn that it's not the penis that makes
the man,
But the man that makes the penis.

# DEAR KAREN

I often think about how someone loved you so
much they wanted to have sex with you, and that
gives me hope that we all can be loved and
wanted just as we are.

Oh Karen,
Your day must've been so hard.
I know that you didn't mean to lash out,
So I'm giving you the benefit of the doubt.

Life isn't easy,
You would know.
There's always drama everywhere you go.
I wish I could ease your jangled nerves,
But you don't want my kind around your curves.

If you knew how I felt when you snapped at me,
I know you wouldn't have done it.
You would have lowered your voice,
And I wouldn't have to be punished—
For your own unhappiness.

I was down today,
And then you walked in.
A confrontation I wasn't expecting.

You have hurt me today.
All because you didn't get your way.

But what I want to know is,
Who hurt you, Karen?
What stole your zest,
And left you barren?

You are someone's daughter.
A misguided angel.
But you came here in anger,
Your attitude disdainful.

What did I do to deserve your venom?
A poisonous snake encased in stretch denim.
At least you are comfortable.

You glared at me Karen,
Your eyes are knives.
Blunt and lacklustre,
Old, no shine.

# RETAIL BLUES

My soul has been sucked.
Shoppers who don't care for my happiness,
Flock the racks,
Spend their stacks.
But my spirit feels flat.

No discounts at the moment,
But they always ask.
I need a break from people,
So I focus on a task.

I'm just asking you how you are,
I'm not trying to sell to you.
It's clear you don't like me,
And I don't like you too.

"I'm just looking" is their favourite line but,
I was just enquiring about their wellbeing.
Sometimes I wonder if I'm chopped liver,
Or a human being.

My feet hurt,
But I plant them and serve.
Trying to beat a budget,
And stay ahead of the curve.

Boss breathing down my neck,
But my back hurts.
I'm doing my best,
But I'm overworked.

I need lunch,
But I can't get away.
A strident woman is walking my way.
I've gone above and beyond with my service,
But I wish they would increase my pay.

# NOT THAT DEEP

Accompanying a shit quote with a pretty picture
doesn't make the words make more sense.
I see what you're trying to do,
But your execution is nonsense.

Half thought metaphors meant for untrained
ears,
and intended for the shallow mind,
make great veils for the vapid kinds.

Posting inspiration like you're some sage,
When you're stuck stealing words right off a
page;
What the fuck?—
I can't even begin to hide my rage.

BUT PEOPLE EAT THIS UP!
That's the thing,
I'm not over criticising,
I just don't think it's good enough.

Words that come with imagery,
But I don't know what I'm seeing,
I struggle to see the symmetry,
And I don't know what you're meaning.

# KFC PT. II

I remember unwrapping you,
And you were stacked.
Towering over me,
You teased me with your meat.
I recall telling you right then and there,
That I was ready to eat.

They said it was all too much for one person,
And I said back to them "Speak for yourself."
They tried to knock you,
And say you're bad for my health.

When I see you,
I'm salacious,
I just want a taste.
I bite you and get you all over my face.

Your secret menu is blessed,
I drag you down for the best.
They say you're so overrated,
But I say I'm just so obsessed.

I wanna pop you in my mouth.
I know it sounds corny,
But when I think about your flavour;

I just get so...hungry.

I could never shake you,
I've tried it before.
You're just so well blended,
I feel you down to my core.

I swear they're all so salty,
Because I found love.
But I guess you can't please everybody,
When push comes to shove.

They say you never dress up for me,
And I say "take that back."
They've just never seen you fresh off the rack.

They say they'll never get it,
But I always do.
Because at the end of the day,
You're my favourite food.

# NEW MANAGER

I used to like my job before you came along.
You lazy cow.
Grazing on the shop floor,
Doing nothing at all,
But getting on my nerves,
And getting all the benefits.

Somehow you got the job with your 8 year old
reference, which you openly brag about with
great confidence.

I hate how you always talk about your work
experience like you're trying to prove yourself,
but you already got the job,
So can you talk about something else?

You came in like the second coming,
Ready to change it all.
A pretentious human being,
You fail to recognise your flaws.

I hate coming to work when I know I'm on with
you,
because I have to work twice as much to do the
things that you don't do.

Things are so bad right now,
That I'm taking work home.
And you constantly invade my thoughts,
When I want to be alone.

# GTFO

I don't want to work with you.
You're a lazy bitch.
Waddling around the store like a duck.
Telling me too much about your sex life.
You sick fuck.
I wish you'd go home early,
I'd rather struggle alone.
You do nothing for me,
You're better off at home.
Don't call me 'babe',
And don't call me 'hun'.
You should know by now,
That I am not the one.

# DEUCES

17

Crowning in bed.
I don't wanna get up.
But something's gotta give,
And I gotta shit.
It's a risk,
But I need the relief.
Even if I never get to sleep.
The stakes have never been so high,
But not listening to my body isn't gonna fly.
Do or die.
Drop the deuce.

# I'M NOT MAD, JUST DISAPPOINTED

Racist white children,
I feel sorry for you.
You were raised by those
who have narrow minds.
The same ones who taught you to be unkind.

Racist white children,
That's not Chinese,
But the language of ignorance you speak.

Your mockery of me speaks volumes,
I'm sorry for your miseducation.
Because we are still connected,
Despite our lack of relation.

I am your neighbour,
Behind the white gates.
Different to the white gates you stand behind,
While fearing what you don't know.

You may have reduced us to a sound,
But my people are a symphony
that you can't silence.
A different answer to your violence.

Your rocks can only be thrown so far,
But you're still hitting nerves.
I remember you,
And all that you were worth.

If the shoe was on the other foot,
I wouldn't blame everything on you.
Death doesn't discriminate,
But ignorant people do.

It's never too late to teach when there's
misinformation trickling down to your children;
That the love they continue to feed the earth will
eventually come back and feed them.

# HAUNT U EVERYDAY

I can't bury this,
Because I don't know if it's really dead.
My memories breathe,
Or is it all in my head?
I tried moving on,
But I can't put this to bed.
I feel so blue,
But my blood's so red.
I'm sorry if I haunt you,
I can have that effect.
If you look in your mirrors,
I don't mean to reflect.
But I guess that's on you,
If I'm still on your mind.
I want to believe you won't forget me in time.

# I'VE SAID ALL I COULD

One moment you were mine,
Then they stole my sunshine.
I can't chase you,
Because my heart is too heavy.
It's going to take some time.
I can't lead you to water,
And make you drink.
You always wanted to be free,
So be it.
I wish that for you everyday.
Even if you can't see it,
I've given you the world.
It's yours to keep,
Even if I'm not in it.

# SOW WHAT?

Everybody leaves,
No roots on trees.
I'm stumped by reality,
But I have to grieve.

If it's your time,
Then fine.
Do what you need.
No more "please, wait, don't";
No more "go—don't leave".

If this is what you need to be grown,
Then go and do that.
Sow your seeds,
Without me.

# I KNOW I WAS GOOD

I know I was good.
For whatever shit he did,
For however the fuck he feels,
Those are the cards that he deals.
But I know I was good.

Good till the end,
I highly recommend me.
5 star girlfriend,
Plus I'm really nice and friendly.

This shit is funny,
You could've been my hunny.
But you went and spent money
on that little ice junkie.

# CALL ME WHEN
# U GET THIS

Beer tastes bad,
But I don't feel good.
This bitterness sucks,
But I've tasted worse.
I need to pee again,
But that's none of your business.
Don't mind me,
I'll be out in a minute.
Locked down and feral,
Am I even human?
All I can sense is peril.
Looming.
Using my words to describe my days,
But all I got is 'shit' 'damn' 'motherfucker'.
I hope that's okay.
I could ask about you,
But I choke on your name.
I'm drowning.
I might sit this one out,
If it's all the same.

# COUPLES COSTUME

Our couples costume didn't get to debut,
Because we've broken up,
And our plans are all screwed.
You were meant to be John,
And I was meant to be Yoko,
But one of us tapped out of Cupid's chokehold.
It's not fair how I seem to care more,
And you're still friends with that awful whore.
Emotionally unavailable,
Your sadness is delayed.
I'm doing my best to be reasonable,
But I can't help but be dismayed.
I feel played.
But it wasn't your intention.
You're just so confused.
And I can't keep waiting for you to come to.
But the memories of everything that we were
meant to do—they haunt me.
I hope they haunt you too.

# MENULAG

My order is late.
Most disappointed I've been to date.
Menulog?
More like Menulag.
You've ruined my night,
And I'm feeling all mad.
Fuck my appetite.
I want my money back.

# NECESSARY

I hate feeling like I've been mean.
A guilty conscious,
I can't wipe clean.
But I'm sorry,
I had to.
I know this doesn't make sense,
But I need this for my self respect.
If you know me,
You'll understand,
And I won't have to explain.
I know you're confused as to what I have to
gain.
But that has to be okay.
I'm not trying to feed you your own medicine.
But this is how it has to end,
for me to begin.

# TRAINWRECK

Moving so fast,
You can't see the signs.
The caffeine is so mean,
Could you maybe slow your roll?
Your head is a jungle,
But your body moves slow.
You have the ideas,
But nothing to show.
You're a compass going crazy,
And your mind could use a map.
You're a lady on a mission,
But what mission is that?
You could stop this train.
Get off and get on again,
Or go home,
And reset.

# THINGS THAT SCARE ME (IN NO PARTICULAR ORDER)

That there won't be a confirmation page before
placing an order on something,
And then paying for something that I wasn't
fully sure of.
Someone that I care about not having any
self-love.

Having someone misconstrue my intentions or
misunderstand me.
Starting to fall when I'm just standing.

Being locked into something that I can't get out
of, or is difficult to cancel or reverse. Leaving a
situation unresolved, where all parties are
feeling terse.

Running into an ex friend who I have nothing to say to, but who wants to engage with me and I have to see it through.

Getting in trouble at work because a customer was being an asshole,
and management won't take my side.
Being so far away from home,
And not being able to find a ride.

That someone will overhear me listening to a sexually explicit Prince song with lots of moaning and think I'm watching porn.
Walking around with total confidence when the seat of my pants are completely torn.

Holding someone else's baby.

Making eye contact with someone through the door crack of a public toilet cubicle. Using hand sanitiser when there's a tear in my cuticle.

Discovering a spider near my face while I'm travelling in a car and not being able to get away because I'm going down a busy road.

Walking down the middle of stairs and falling because there's nothing to hold.

Finding that there are missing pieces of chicken from my KFC order, but I just got home.

Being racially attacked while I'm out alone.